Step-by-Step Excercises to
BUILD STRONG WRITING SKILLS
for Success in School and Beyond

When IN DOUBT Leave IT OUT

DR. CHRISHUNA HARRIS-GRIFFIN

When In Doubt, Leave It Out
© 2025 Dr. Chrishuna Harris-Griffin
All rights reserved. No part of this publication may be reproduced, distributed, or transmitted in any form or by any means, including photocopying, recording, or other electronic or mechanical methods, without the prior written permission of the publisher, except in the case of brief quotations used in critical reviews or certain other noncommercial uses permitted by copyright law.

Published by Morgan Hale Studios, LLC
Atlanta, Georgia
info@MorganHaleStudios.com

Author website: www.WritingWithDrChrissy.com
Illustrations by Morgan Hale

ISBN: 979-8-218-72082-7
Printed in the United States of America
First Edition, 2025

Purpose & Inspiration

I wrote When in Doubt, Leave It Out to empower students, the educators who support them, and anyone seeking to write with clarity and confidence. Strong writing skills open doors to academic success and future professional opportunities, yet so many people struggle to express their ideas effectively.

This guide is designed to offer simple, practical strategies that make writing less intimidating and more powerful. Inside, you'll find easy-to-follow tips to help you avoid common mistakes, improve clarity, and develop a polished, purposeful writing style. My goal is to give every reader tools that build confidence, strengthen communication, and inspire a love for writing.

The title, When in Doubt, Leave It Out, was inspired by a simple principle I found myself repeating to students and colleagues: when you are unsure about a word—its meaning, its spelling, or its usage—it's better to leave it out and choose a clearer, more familiar alternative. This approach eliminates confusion, keeps your writing clean and precise, and reminds us that effective communication doesn't have to be complicated—it just has to be clear.

Testimonies

Dr. Chrishuna Harris-Griffin, affectionately known as "Chrissy", is my only daughter, whom I am very proud of. As a little girl Chrissy required me to read to her no matter how late it was or how exhausted I was. Chrissy has always had a passion for writing and reading, however writing is her favorite. Growing up, she had to have numerous of books and notepads to read to her many dolls and would drilled them until she felt they earned an "A". I can recall buying her a journal every year for Christmas and she would need new paper by January. I am elated that Chrissy is fulfilling one of her many desires. Her father, the late Sammie Harris Jr. would be peacock proud and hyena happy. Chrissy, I am so proud of you and keep soaring.

- Love always, your mother,
Pearl Bell-Harris.

I'm beyond ecstatic for Chrishuna having her 1st book published! Since we were young school age girls, you have been so eloquent when it comes to pen to pad Whatever message you wanted to convey came across crystal clearly in essays and speeches as I know it's going to in your book! Endless congratulations to continued success!

- Leslie "Chelle" Poston

Dr. Chrishuna Griffin is an exceptional writer whose impeccable skill and versatility truly set her apart. Whether crafting academic papers, creative fiction, professional content, or persuasive narratives, she consistently delivers work of the highest quality. Her ability to adapt seamlessly across genres is nothing short of remarkable. What truly distinguishes Dr. Griffin, beyond her talent , is her professionalism. She is highly organized, efficient, and meets every deadline with precision. Collaborating with her is always a smooth, rewarding experience. I wholeheartedly recommend Dr. Griffin to anyone in need of outstanding writing delivered with excellence and integrity.

- Dr. Terri North-Byrts

When I was a child, I hated writing! I felt as though I never had the skills and guidance to write about how I felt or summarized papers. That changed when I was introduced to Dr. Griffin. Working with Dr. Griffin has truly transformed the way I approach writing. Her guidance and support have helped me grow not only as a writer but as a communicator. She didn't just correct my work, Dr. Griffin taught me how to think critically, organize my thoughts, and express them with clarity and confidence. The skills I've learned from Dr. Griffin are tools I'll carry with me for the rest of my life. Her passion for teaching and dedication to her students made all the difference, and I'm incredibly grateful for everything she's poured into helping me succeed.

- Vicky S Robinson

Preface

I have been writing this guide for two years. However, in many ways, it began years ago, as my passion for writing began at an early age. Reflecting on my childhood, I recall writing on various topics and formats using my chalk board. I have decided to create this short guide to assist those who may be encountering challenges with writing essays, proposals, thesis, dissertation and basic papers. Over the past 20 years, I have had the privilege of working with both nontraditional and traditional students, helping them gain the confidence to become proficient writers. However, I have observed that they all share a common need: the ability to apply fundamental grammatical principles. This material is a straightforward read and serves as an informative guide, so please take a moment to relax and have confidence in your abilities.

When IN DOUBT Leave IT OUT

Table of Contents

Introduction to Basics..	9
Parts of Speech..	10
Spelling Fundamentals...	13
Punctuation: The Road Signs of Writing......................................	16
Uncountable Nouns (No "S," Please!)..	18
Common Uncountable Noun Errors...	19
Word Confusion: Homophones...	21
More Commonly Confused Word Pairs..	22
Introduction to Figurative Language...	24
Types of Figurative Language, Part 1..	25
Types of Figurative Language, Part 2..	28
Types of Figurative Language, Part 3..	31
Easy Essays: Getting Started..	33
Crafting a Strong Thesis Statement..	35
Developing Body Paragraphs..	39
Writing Effective Introductions and Conclusions.................	42
Essay Structure: Putting It All Together.......................................	46
Essay Writing Process...	48
Revising and Editing Your Writing..	51
Conclusion: You've Got This!...	55
Answer Key (Activities 1–24)...	56

Introduction to the Basics

Before we can write with clarity and confidence, we must revisit the foundations. Think back to elementary school: capital letters, punctuation, and spelling were the building blocks of every sentence. Those basics still matter—whether you're sending an email, writing a report, creating a resume, or helping your child with homework.

Strong writing begins with understanding the essential components that make up our language. These fundamental elements form the framework upon which all effective communication is built. By mastering these basics, you'll develop the confidence to express your thoughts clearly and precisely in any context.

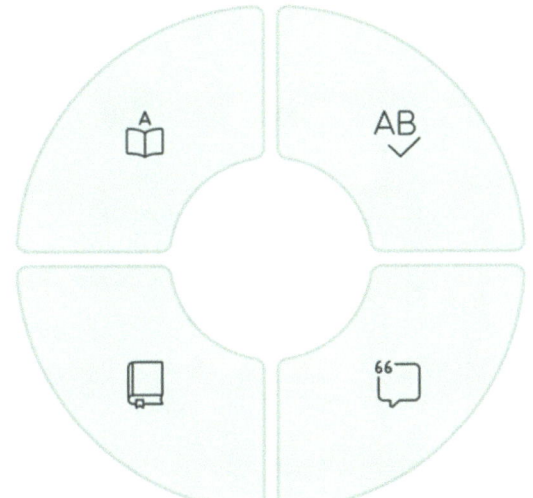

Grammar

The system and structure of a language, including rules for forming sentences and combining words

Spelling

The correct arrangement of letters to form words according to accepted usage

Vocabulary

The body of words used in a particular language or context

Punctuation

Marks that clarify meaning and indicate how text should be read

This chapter will refresh these skills and give you hands-on practice so you can write effectively and with ease. We'll explore each component in detail, providing examples and exercises to reinforce your understanding. By the end of this section, you'll have a solid foundation upon which to build more advanced writing skills.

Notes:
_____
_____
_____
_____
_____
_____
_____

Parts of Speech

Knowing the parts of speech will help you structure sentences correctly. Each word in the English language serves a specific grammatical function. Understanding these functions is essential for constructing clear, effective sentences.

Verbs

Words that show action or occurrence.

- Express physical actions (run, jump, write)
- Describe mental activities (think, understand)
- Indicate states of being (am, is, are)

Examples: color, cry, laugh, dance, pray

Nouns

Words that name a person, place, thing, or idea.

- Common: general names (store, aunt, actor)
- Collective: group names (team, family, crew)
- Proper: specific names, always capitalized (Maria, Texas)
- Abstract: intangible concepts (love, courage, strength)

Adjectives

Words that describe or modify nouns or pronouns.

- Describe qualities (beautiful, happy, brave)
- Indicate quantity (many, few, three)
- Specify which one (this, that, those)

Adverbs

Words that describe verbs, adjectives, or other adverbs.

- Tell how (quickly, softly)
- Tell when (often, recently)
- Tell where (here, everywhere)
- Tell to what extent (very, extremely)

The remaining parts of speech play equally important roles in constructing meaningful sentences:

Pronouns	**Conjunctions**	**Prepositions**	**Interjections**
Words that replace nouns to avoid repetition.	Words that connect other words or groups of words.	Words that show relationships between words.	Words that express emotion.
- Personal: he, she, they, we, you - Possessive: mine, yours, theirs - Relative: who, which, that	- Coordinating: and, but, or - Subordinating: because, although, when - Correlative: either/or, neither/nor	- Location: in, on, under - Direction: to, toward, from - Time: at, during, before	- Exclamations: Wow!, Oh!, Hey! - Often followed by exclamation points - Usually stand alone or at beginning of sentence

> Understanding parts of speech allows you to analyze sentences, identify grammatical errors, and construct more varied and sophisticated writing. Practice identifying these elements in your everyday reading to reinforce your understanding.

✏️ Activity 1: Fill-in-the-Blank Story

Directions: Fill in each blank with the correct part of speech (noun, verb, adjective, adverb, etc.). Then read your silly story out loud!

Yesterday, my _____ (adjective) _____ (noun) decided to _____ (verb) all the way to _____ (place).

On the way, we saw a _____ (adjective) _____ (animal) that could _____ (verb) _____ (adverb)!

I shouted, "_____!" (interjection) and ran _____ (preposition) the _____ (noun).

It was the most _____ (adjective) day ever!

✏️ Activity 2: Practicing the Remaining Parts of Speech

Directions: Read each sentence carefully. Fill in the blank or underline the correct word to show your understanding of pronouns, conjunctions, prepositions, and interjections.

1. Pronouns: Replace the underlined noun with the correct pronoun.

<u>Maria and I</u> saw Maria's little brother at the park. → _____

2. Prepositions: Circle the correct preposition and then fill in the blank.

The cat is hiding _____ the bed. (in / before / toward)

3. Conjunctions: Circle the correct conjunction and then fill in the blank.

I wanted to go to the party, _____ I had to finish my homework first. (and / but / because)

4. Interjections: Choose the best interjection to complete the sentence. Fill in the blank.

_____! That rollercoaster ride was amazing! (Hey / Wow / Because)

ⓘ 5. Mixed Practice: Underline the pronoun, circle the conjunction, and box the preposition in this sentence:

- *She wanted to join the soccer team, but her practice was at the same time as band rehearsal.*

Spelling Fundamentals

Spelling matters. Incorrect spelling can confuse your reader or change your meaning entirely. In today's world of spell-check and autocorrect, it's still important to understand spelling principles and recognize common errors.

One of the most challenging aspects of English spelling involves homophones—words that sound alike but have different meanings and spellings. Mixing these up is a common error even among native speakers.

Common Homophone Pairs

bare / bear	Without covering / animal
brake / break	To stop / to separate into pieces
cell / sell	Small room or unit / to exchange for money
hear / here	To perceive sound / in this place
principal / principle	School leader or main / fundamental truth
weather / whether	Atmospheric conditions / expressing alternatives

English Spelling Rules

- "I before E except after C" (believe, receive)
- Words ending in silent E drop the E before adding suffixes beginning with vowels (hope → hoping)
- Words ending in Y preceded by a consonant change Y to I before adding most suffixes (happy → happier)
- Words ending in a consonant double that consonant before adding a suffix beginning with a vowel (run → running)

✏️ Activity 3: Homophone Match-Ups

Directions: Read the sentence carefully. Write the correct homophone in the blank. Each word can only be used once.

Word Bank:
bare • bear • brake • break • cell • sell • hear • here • principal • principle • weather • whether

1. Please do not _____ the chair; it is already wobbly.
2. The mountain _____ looked scary, but it walked away into the woods.
3. Always use your seatbelt and press the _____ when the light turns red.
4. My cousin wants to _____ her bike at the yard sale.
5. The prisoner was locked in a small _____.
6. Can you _____ the music playing outside?
7. The library is over _____ next to the park.
8. Our school _____ gave a speech at the assembly.
9. Honesty is an important life _____.
10. Tomorrow's _____ forecast calls for sunshine.
11. I couldn't decide _____ to go to the park or stay home.
12. She walked on the cold floor with her _____ feet.

👉 **Extension Challenge:** Write **one original sentence** using any homophone pair from the list. Underline the homophones you used.

_____

Improving your spelling skills requires regular practice and attention. Here are some strategies to help:

Read extensively—exposure to correctly spelled words reinforces proper spelling

- Keep a personal dictionary of words you frequently misspell
- Study word patterns and roots to understand spelling logic
- Use mnemonic devices to remember tricky spellings
- Practice writing by hand, which engages different cognitive processes than typing

Remember that while spell-checking tools are helpful, they won't catch all errors, especially with homophones. Developing strong spelling skills remains an important part of clear, effective writing.

✏️ Activity 4: Build Your Spelling Power

Directions: Use the strategies you just learned to strengthen your spelling skills. Complete each section by writing in the workbook.

1	**Tricky word: because** • Mnemonic: *Big Elephants Can Always Understand Small Elephants (B.E.C.A.U.S.E)*
2	**Tricky word: friend** • Mnemonic: *I will be your friEND to the END*
3	**Tricky word: <u>Wednesday</u>** • My mnemonic: _____
4	**Tricky word: _____** • My mnemonic: _____

Punctuation: The Road Signs of Writing

Punctuation shows the reader how to read your sentences and where to pause, stop, or change tone. Just as road signs guide drivers, punctuation marks guide readers through your text. Understanding how to use these marks correctly is essential for clear communication. Let's explore the 14 common punctuation marks and their functions:

Terminal Punctuation

- **Period (.)** - Ends a statement or command
- **Question Mark (?)** - Ends a direct question
- **Exclamation Point (!)** - Expresses strong emotion

Internal Punctuation

- **Comma (,)** - Separates elements in a sentence
- **Semicolon (;)** - Connects related independent clauses
- **Colon (:)** - Introduces lists or explanations

Paired Punctuation

- **Parentheses ( )** - Enclose supplementary information
- **Brackets [ ]** - Enclose clarifications within quotes
- **Quotation Marks (" ")** - Indicate direct speech

✏️ Activity 5: Choose the Right Road Sign

Directions: Read each sentence. Choose the correct punctuation mark (period, question mark, exclamation point, comma, semicolon, colon, parentheses, brackets, quotation marks) and write it in the blank.

1. I love reading exciting books ___
2. Can you help me with this math problem ___
3. I packed my bag with pencils___ erasers___ and paper.
4. We have two choices___ stay home or go to the park.
5. I'm not sure we should go out tonight ___ it looks like rain.
6. My brother (who is younger than me) wants to come along ___
7. She said___ "I can't wait to see the movie."
8. The reporter wrote that the storm would arrive [on Thursday] and last all weekend ___

Common Punctuation Errors and Corrections

Error	Correction	Example
Comma splice	Use period, semicolon, or conjunction	❌ I love writing, it's my favorite hobby. ✅ I love writing; it's my favorite hobby.
Missing comma after introductory element	Add comma	❌ After dinner we went for a walk. ✅ After dinner, we went for a walk.
Misused apostrophe	Use for possession or contraction, not plurals	❌ The Smith's are coming to dinner. ✅ The Smiths are coming to dinner.
Overuse of exclamation points	Use sparingly for true emphasis	❌ I'm so excited to see you!!!!! ✅ I'm so excited to see you!

Proper punctuation enhances readability and precision. When you use punctuation correctly, your writing flows naturally and your meaning becomes clearer. Take time to master these marks—they're small but mighty tools in effective writing.

✏️ Activity 6: Fix the Punctuation!

Directions: Rewrite each sentence correctly.

1. After school we played basketball in the driveway.
   _____

2. The teacher said "Please put your books away."
   _____

3. My cousins are here!!!!!
   _____

Uncountable Nouns: No "S" Please!

Some nouns in English are uncountable—you can't make them plural by adding "s." These words represent concepts, categories, or items that aren't counted individually in English.

Singular Form Only

Uncountable nouns use singular verb forms

Example: The information **is** helpful. (Not "are")

No Indefinite Article

Don't use "a" or "an" with uncountable nouns

Example: I need advice. (Not "an advice")

Use Quantity Words

Use "some," "much," "a lot of" instead

Example: I have some homework.

Use Container Words

Use units of measurement when needed

Example: Three pieces of furniture

Common Uncountable Nouns by Category

Remember that some nouns can be both countable and uncountable depending on context. For example, "time" is uncountable when referring to the concept (I don't have time) but countable when referring to specific instances (I've been there three times).

Category	Examples
Abstractions	advice, information, research, news, progress, evidence, luck
Materials	furniture, equipment, clothing, jewelry, machinery, luggage,
Liquids	water, coffee, milk, oil, blood, gasoline, soup
Foods	rice, bread, pasta, cheese, meat, fish, fruit (general)
Activities	homework, work, travel, fun, sleep, research, weather

Common Uncountable Noun Errors

Uncountable nouns are words we cannot count as individual items because they describe substances, concepts, or groups that are seen as a whole, not as separate units. For example, we don't say *"informations"* or *"advices"*—instead, we say *"information"* and *"advice."* If we want to count them, we use phrases like *"a piece of information"* or *"two pieces of advice."*

The same is true for words like *furniture, luggage, homework, bread, traffic,* and *music.* These nouns always stay singular, even when they mean "a lot." Instead of saying *"furnitures,"* we say *"furniture."* Instead of *"homeworks,"* we say *"homework."* Learning these patterns helps avoid common errors and makes sentences clearer.

Incorrect Pluralization

❌ ~~The teacher gave me many useful advices.~~

✅ The teacher gave me a lot of useful advice.

Incorrect Articles

❌ ~~I need a permission to enter the building.~~

✅ I need permission to enter the building.

Wrong Verb Agreement

❌ ~~The furniture in my house are very old.~~

✅ The furniture in my house is very old.

Missing Measurement Words

❌ ~~I bought new equipment for my office.~~

✅ I bought new pieces of equipment for my office.

> ### ⓘ Quantity Expressions for Uncountable Nouns
>
> When you need to express quantity with uncountable nouns, use:
>
> - **General:** some, a little, a lot of, much, any
> - **Specific units:** a piece of, an item of, a bit of
> - **Containers:** a bottle of, a cup of, a spoonful of

✏️ Activity 7: Correcting Uncountable Noun Errors

> ⓘ Example:

Incorrect Sentence	Corrected Sentence
We bought three new ~~furnitures~~ for the office.	We bought three <u>new pieces of furniture</u> for the office.
I need more ~~equipments~~ for the project.	I need <u>more equipment</u> for the project.
The staffs ~~are~~ working overtime this week.	The staff <u>is</u> working overtime this week.
He gave me ~~many useful informations.~~	He gave me <u>a lot of useful information.</u>

Review the following sentences and identify the errors with uncountable nouns. Cross out the errors and rewrite the sentence correctly on the line.

Incorrect Sentence	Corrected Sentence
She baked three breads for the picnic.	_____
He gave me some very helpful homeworks.	_____
We heard many beautiful musics at the festival.	_____
The traffics on the road were heavy today.	_____
I need to pack my luggages for the trip.	_____

Word Confusion: Homophones

Sometimes less is more. If you're unsure about a word or phrase, it's often better to choose a simple, familiar term instead of something uncommon or confusing. Clear writing is always the goal—selecting the right words makes your message stronger and easier to understand.

Homophones, words that sound alike but have different meanings and spellings, are among the most common sources of confusion in English writing. Let's explore some frequently confused pairs.

Are vs. Our

Are: A form of the verb "to be"

Example: We are going to Atlanta next Friday.

Our: Shows possession

Example: Is that our dog running down the street?

Its vs. It's

Its: Shows possession

Example: The city has its own charm.

It's: Contraction for "it is" or "it has"

Example: It's going to rain today.

Effect vs. Affect

Effect: Usually a noun; the result

Example: The new law had a positive effect on businesses.

Affect: Usually a verb; to influence

Example: Will this decision affect your schedule?

1. Their

Their - Shows possession

Example: The students forgot their books.

2. There

There - Refers to a place

Example: Put the box over there.

3. They're

They're - Contraction for "they are"

Example: They're coming to dinner tonight.

Mastering these distinctions takes practice, but understanding the difference between commonly confused words will significantly improve your writing clarity. When in doubt, take a moment to verify the correct usage—your readers will appreciate the precision.

More Commonly Confused Word Pairs

English contains many word pairs that cause confusion due to similar spellings or pronunciations. Learning to distinguish between these pairs will help you avoid common errors in your writing.

Accept vs. Except

Accept: To receive willingly

Example: I accept your apology.

Except: Excluding; other than

Example: Everyone came except John.

Your vs. You're

Your: Shows possession

Example: Is this your book?

You're: Contraction of "you are"

Example: You're going to be late.

Weather vs. Whether

Weather: Atmospheric conditions

Example: The weather is beautiful today.

Whether: Expressing alternatives

Example: I don't know whether to go or stay.

Than vs. Then

Than: Used for comparison

Example: She is taller than her brother.

Then: Refers to time

Example: We ate dinner, then watched a movie.

Lose vs. Loose

Lose: To misplace or not win

Example: Don't lose your keys.

Loose: Not tight; free

Example: The screw is loose.

Principal vs. Principle

Principal: Main person or sum of money

Example: The school principal spoke at assembly.

Principle: Fundamental truth or belief

Example: She lives by her principles.

📒 Memory Tips for Commonly Confused Words

- **Affect/Effect:** *A*ffect is usually an *A*ction (verb); *E*ffect is usually the *E*nd result (noun)
- **Your/You're:** If you can replace it with "you are," use "you're"
- **Its/It's:** If you can replace it with "it is" or "it has," use "it's"
- **Their/There/They're:** "There" contains "here" - both refer to place
- **Principal/Principle:** The school principal is your "pal"

When you're uncertain about which word to use, take a moment to check. The extra time spent verifying correct usage will result in clearer, more professional writing. Remember, spell-check won't always catch these errors since both words are spelled correctly—it's up to you

✏️ Activity 8: Homophone Challenge

Directions: Circle the correct word in each sentence.

We **(are / our)** going to the zoo tomorrow.	The cat chased **(its / it's)** tail in circles.	The loud noise did not **(effect / affect)** me at all.
Please put your shoes over **(their / there / they're)**.	**(Their / There / They're)** learning about the Bible at church today.	She **(knew / new)** the song by heart.
I want to **(write / right)** a letter to my friend.	We saw a **(pair / pear)** of birds on the fence.	Please don't **(waist / waste)** your food.

The sun will **(sea / see)** us through the window.

Introduction to Figurative Language

Figurative language makes writing more vivid, persuasive, and engaging. It uses comparisons, imagery, and expressions to create deeper meaning beyond the literal words on the page. When used effectively, figurative language can transform ordinary writing into something memorable and impactful.

Unlike literal language, which means exactly what it says, figurative language creates connections between different ideas or images.

Simile

Compares using "like" or "as"

Example: Her smile is like sunshine on a cloudy day.

Imagery

Language that appeals to the senses

Ex: The tangy scent of autumn leaves filled the air.

Symbolism

Using objects to represent abstract ideas

Ex: The dove represented peace in the painting.

Metaphor

Direct comparison without "like" or "as"

Ex: His words were daggers to my heart.

Personification

Gives human traits to non-human things

Ex: The wind whispered through the trees.

Hyperbole

Extreme exaggeration for emphasis

Ex: I'm so hungry I could eat a horse.

Figurative language serves several important purposes in writing:

> ⓘ Practice incorporating figurative language purposefully. Do not confuse readers with overly complex sentences.

- ☐ **Creates vivid images** that help readers visualize concepts
- ☐ **Explains complex ideas** by relating them to familiar concepts
- ☐ **Adds emotional impact** to make writing more memorable
- ☐ **Engages readers** by inviting them to make connections
- ☐ **Adds layers of meaning** that enrich the reading experience

Types of Figurative Language: Part 1

Let's explore several types of figurative language in more detail, with examples and tips for using them effectively in your writing.

Simile

A simile compares two different things using the words "like" or "as" to show how they are similar in one specific way.

> Her eyes sparkled like diamonds.
>
> The child was as quiet as a mouse.
>
> Working with him is like trying to nail jelly to a wall.

Effective similes create clear, vivid images by comparing something unfamiliar or abstract to something more concrete and familiar. They work best when the comparison is unexpected yet apt.

Metaphor

A metaphor states that one thing is another, creating a direct comparison without using "like" or "as." Metaphors suggest a deeper connection than similes.

> The classroom was a zoo.
>
> Her voice is music to my ears.
>
> Time is money.

Strong metaphors make readers see familiar things in new ways or help them understand abstract concepts through concrete images. Extended metaphors develop the comparison throughout a paragraph or entire piece.

Notes:

_____
_____
_____
_____
_____
_____
_____
_____
_____

Onomatopoeia

Words that imitate the sounds they describe

- The bees buzzed around the flowers
- The bacon sizzled in the pan
- The door creaked open slowly

Personification

Giving human qualities to non-human things

- The wind whispered secrets to the trees
- The stars winked at me from the sky
- Fear knocked at the door of my heart

Hyperbole

Extreme exaggeration for emphasis or humor

- I'm so hungry I could eat a horse
- I've told you a million times
- Her smile lit up the entire city

Oxymoron

Combining contradictory words

- Deafening silence
- Original copy
- Jumbo shrimp

When incorporating figurative language into your writing, aim for balance. Too little, and your writing may feel flat; too much, and it may seem forced or confusing. Choose figurative language that enhances your message and resonates with your audience.

✏️ Activity 9: Figurative Language Match-Up

Directions: Draw a line from the figurative language type in Column A to the correct example in Column B.

Onomatopoeia	A. I've told you a million times.
Personification	B. The bacon sizzled in the pan.
Hyperbole	C. Jumbo Shrimp
Oxymoron	D. The stars winked at me from the sky.

✏️ Activity 10: Figurative Language Makeover

Directions: Rewrite each boring sentence using the type of figurative language shown in parentheses. Be creative!

1. The dog ran fast. *(Simile)*
   → _____

2. The storm was loud. *(Personification)*
   → _____

3. My backpack is heavy. *(Hyperbole)*
   → _____

4. The girl was very kind. *(Metaphor)*
   → _____

5. The candle burned in the dark room. *(Imagery)*
   → _____

👉 **Extension Challenge:** Pick one of your new sentences and **draw a picture** that shows the figurative language in the box below.

Types of Figurative Language: Part 2

Let's continue exploring additional types of figurative language that can enhance your writing.

Allusion

An indirect reference to a well-known person, place, event, or literary work

- He was a real Romeo when it came to romance.
- Her solution to the problem was her Achilles' heel.
- The new policy opened a Pandora's box of complications.

Idiom

An expression whose meaning differs from the literal meaning of its words

- Barking up the wrong tree (pursuing a mistaken course of action)
- Break the ice (reduce tension in a social situation)
- Hit the nail on the head (describe exactly what is causing a situation)

Imagery

Language that appeals to the senses to create mental pictures

- The warm, buttery aroma of freshly baked cookies filled the kitchen.
- The sharp, metallic taste of blood lingered in his mouth.
- The fabric felt rough and scratchy against her skin.

Symbolism

Using an object, person, situation, or word to represent something else, often an abstract idea

- The dove symbolizes peace
- The red rose represents love and passion
- The broken chain symbolizes freedom from oppression

> Effective symbolism often builds on cultural associations but can also establish new connections within a specific piece of writing.

Irony:

A contrast between expectation and reality

Verbal irony: Saying the opposite of what you mean

Ex: "What lovely weather we're having," during a thunderstorm.

Situational irony: When the outcome is contrary to expectation

Ex: A fire station burning down.

Dramatic irony: When the audience knows things that the characters don't

Ex: The audience knows there's a bomb under the table, while the characters are eating, unaware.

✏️ Activity 11: Irony Investigator Worksheet

Directions: Read the passage below carefully. Underline the examples of **irony** you find. Then, in the boxes provided, label each one as **verbal irony, situational irony, or dramatic irony.**

It was the day of the big fire-safety assembly, and the students were gathered in the gym. The principal proudly announced, *"This is the safest school in the district!"* Just then, the fire alarm blared—because someone had burned popcorn in the teacher's lounge.

Later at lunch, Mia spilled juice all over her new white shirt and muttered, *"Well, aren't I the picture of grace?"* Her friends couldn't help laughing.

That evening, while studying for her spelling test, she proudly told her mom, *"I can't possibly miss a single word tomorrow."* The very first word on the test was *irony*—and she spelled it wrong.

Identify the Irony

1. Sentence: _____
   Type of Irony: ▎Verbal ▎Situational ▎Dramatic

2. Sentence: _____
   Type of Irony: ▎Verbal ▎Situational ▎Dramatic

3. Sentence: _____
   Type of Irony: ▎Verbal ▎Situational ▎Dramatic

✏️ Activity 12: Figurative Language Detective Story

Directions: Read the short story below. Underline the figurative language you find. Then label each one (Allusion, Idiom, Imagery, Symbolism, or Irony).

> It was the first day of school, and Jordan wanted to break the ice with his new classmates.
> When he saw Sarah smile, he thought, *"Wow, she's like a modern-day Cinderella."*
> The classroom was filled with the smell of fresh crayons and the scratch of pencils on paper.
>
> On the teacher's desk stood a bright apple, a symbol of learning and knowledge.
> At lunch, Jordan spilled his drink and laughed, "Well, isn't this the perfect day?" even though it clearly wasn't.

👉 **Extension Challenge:** Write one more sentence to add to the story using figurative language of your choice.

_____

_____

✏️ Activity 13: Figurative Language Flip Game

Directions: Below are "plain" sentences. Rewrite each one to make it stronger by adding figurative language. The type you must use is given in parentheses.

1. The boy was very strong. *(Allusion)*
   → _____

2. She was nervous about giving a speech. *(Idiom)*
   → _____

3. The soup was hot. *(Imagery)*
   → _____

4. The broken clock sat on the shelf. *(Symbolism)*
   → _____

5. It rained during the picnic. *(Irony)*
   → _____

Types of Figurative Language: Part 3

Let's complete our exploration of figurative language by examining some additional techniques that can add sophistication and impact to your writing.

Alliteration

Repetition of the same consonant sound at the beginning of nearby words

- Peter Piper picked a peck of pickled peppers.
- She sells seashells by the seashore.
- Wild and wooly wombats wandered aimlessly.

Alliteration creates rhythm and emphasizes key words, making phrases more memorable. It's particularly effective in titles, slogans, and poetry.

Pun

A play on words that exploits multiple meanings or similar-sounding words

- I used to be a baker, but I couldn't make enough dough.
- Time flies like an arrow; fruit flies like a banana.
- I'm reading a book about anti-gravity. It's impossible to put down!

Puns add humor and cleverness to writing but should be used sparingly in formal contexts.

Litotes

Understated expression using double negatives to affirm a positive

- That's not a bad idea. (It's a good idea)
- He's not unintelligent. (He's smart)
- The presentation wasn't unsuccessful. (It was successful)

Litotes creates a moderate tone and can be used for understatement or ironic emphasis.

Anaphora

Repetition of a word or phrase at the beginning of successive clauses

- I have a dream that one day... I have a dream that my four children... I have a dream today! (Martin Luther King Jr.)
- Every day, every hour, every minute we must resist.
- Never give in, never give up, never surrender.

Anaphora creates a strong rhythmic effect and emphasizes key ideas through repetition.

Synecdoche

Using a part to represent the whole or vice versa

- All hands on deck! (referring to sailors)
- The White House announced new policies. (referring to the U.S. presidential administration)
- He's just hired some new brains for the project. (referring to intelligent people)

Metonymy

Referring to something by something closely associated with it

- The pen is mightier than the sword. (writing vs. military force)
- Hollywood released a new blockbuster. (the film industry)
- The crown issued a statement. (the monarchy)

> ⓘ **Using Figurative Language Effectively**
>
> - **Choose purposefully:** Select techniques that enhance your specific message
> - **Consider your audience:** Ensure your references will be understood
> - **Aim for originality:** Avoid clichés and overly familiar expressions
> - **Use moderation:** Too much figurative language can overwhelm readers
> - **Revise critically:** Ask if each instance truly strengthens your writing

Figurative language transforms ordinary writing into something memorable and impactful. As you practice these techniques, you'll develop a natural sense for when and how to incorporate them effectively in your own unique voice.

✏️ Activity 14: Figurative Language Fill-in-the-Blank

Directions: Complete each sentence using your imagination so it fits the figurative language type.

1. (Alliteration) The silly _____ sang songs on Sunday.
2. (Pun) I used to be a teacher, but I lost my _____.
3. (Litotes) That's not the _____ cake I've ever tasted.
4. (Anaphora) I will _____. I will _____. I will _____.
5. (Synecdoche) All _____ on deck!
6. (Alliteration) The bouncing _____ baked bread by the brook.
7. (Pun) I used to be a gardener, but my business didn't _____.

Easy Essays: Getting Started

Writing an essay doesn't have to feel overwhelming. Every essay follows a clear structure that, once mastered, provides a reliable framework for expressing your ideas. Understanding this structure will help you approach essay writing with confidence.

Introduction

Introduces the topic and your main idea

- Opens with an attention-grabbing hook
- Provides necessary background information
- Ends with a clear thesis statement

Body Paragraphs

At least three paragraphs, each with one main point

- Begins with a topic sentence
- Includes evidence and examples
- Explains how evidence supports your thesis
- Contains at least 5 complete sentences

Conclusion

Summarizes your main points and restates your position

- Restates thesis in different words
- Summarizes key points from body paragraphs
- Ends with a thought-provoking final statement

Choosing a Topic

If you can choose your own topic:

- Pick something that genuinely interests you
- Choose a subject you know well or are excited to research
- Consider current events for timely relevance
- Think about unique perspectives you can offer
- Select a topic with sufficient available research

If your topic is assigned:

- Narrow your focus to a specific angle
- Identify aspects that interest you personally
- Consider different approaches to the topic
- Look for connections to larger themes
- Avoid topics you don't understand or can't research easily

Remember, a good essay topic should be:

Specific enough to cover thoroughly

Interesting to both you and your readers

Debatable with multiple perspectives (for argumentative essays)

Significant enough to matter to your audience

Researchable with available sources and evidence

> ⓘ Taking time to select and refine your topic before you begin writing will save you time and frustration.

✏️ Activity 15: The Big Question

If you had the power to change **one rule, belief, or practice** in your school, community, or even the world, what would it be — and why?

Directions: Think carefully about your answer. Now turn your idea into a strong **essay topic or essay title**. Write the topic on the line below.

Ex: **Big Question Answer →** *I would change the rule that students can't use phones in school.* **Essay Title →** *"Phones in Class: A Tool, Not a Distraction"*

Your Topic: _____

Crafting a Strong Thesis Statement

A thesis statement is the backbone of your essay—it tells readers exactly what you'll be arguing or explaining. An effective thesis statement is specific, debatable, and concise. It typically appears at the end of your introduction and guides the development of your entire essay.

What Makes a Strong Thesis?

- **Specific:** Addresses a narrow, focused topic
- **Clear:** Uses precise language without vague terms
- **Arguable:** Presents a claim others might dispute
- **Significant:** Addresses an important or interesting issue
- **Concise:** Usually one or two sentences

Common Thesis Problems

- **Too broad:** "Social media has many effects on society."
- **Too vague:** "Education is important for several reasons."
- **Merely factual:** "The Earth orbits around the sun."
- **Just an announcement:** "This paper will discuss remote work."
- **Question instead of statement:** "How does climate change affect agriculture?"

✏️ Activity 16: Fix That Thesis!

Directions: Read each weak thesis statement below. Then, rewrite it so that it is **specific, clear, arguable, significant, and concise.**

1. Weak: *Social media has many effects on society.*
   Strong: _____

2. Weak: *Education is important for several reasons.*
   Strong: _____

3. Weak: *The Earth orbits around the sun.*
   Strong: _____

4. Weak: *This paper will discuss remote work.*
   Strong: _____

5. Weak: *How does climate change affect agriculture?*
   Strong: _____

Thesis Statement Formulas

Use these formulas to help structure your thesis statement:

1 Argumentative

Formula: Although [opposing view], [your position] because of [reasons 1, 2, and 3].

Example: Although some believe remote learning is inferior to traditional education, online courses provide valuable educational opportunities because they increase accessibility, offer scheduling flexibility, and develop students' technological literacy.

2 Analytical

Formula: [Subject] [reveals/demonstrates/symbolizes] [insight] through [aspects 1, 2, and 3].

Example: The character of Atticus Finch in "To Kill a Mockingbird" demonstrates moral courage through his defense of Tom Robinson, his interactions with his children, and his responses to community prejudice.

3 Expository

Formula: [Topic] is characterized by [aspects 1, 2, and 3].

Example: Effective leadership is characterized by clear communication, emotional intelligence, and adaptability to change.

Notes:
_____
_____
_____
_____

Thesis Statement Before and After Examples:

Too Broad	Improved
❌ "Technology has changed our lives."	✅ "The widespread adoption of smartphones has fundamentally altered how teenagers socialize, leading to social anxiety, reduced face-to-face communication skills, and vulnerability to cyberbullying."

Too Vague	Improved
❌ "Climate change is bad for the environment."	✅ "Rising global temperatures threaten coral reef ecosystems by causing coral bleaching, disrupting symbiotic relationships, and reducing diversity in marine life.

Example Thesis

"The COVID-19 pandemic had positive effects, including more family time, new business ventures, and the growth of remote work."

This thesis is specific, makes a claim others might dispute, and clearly outlines three main points that will be developed in the body paragraphs.

Crafting an effective thesis statement takes time and revision. Don't expect to write a perfect thesis on your first attempt. Start with a working thesis that captures your main idea, then refine it.

✏️ Activity 17: Thesis Statement Before & After

Directions: Read the "Before" thesis statement, then rewrite it into a stronger, more specific version. Use the examples provided as a guide.

1. Too Broad Before: ***Sports are fun.*** Rewrite a stronger thesis:
   _____

2. Too Vague Before: ***Pollution is a big problem.*** Rewrite a stronger thesis:
   _____

3. Just an Announcement Before: ***This essay will talk about healthy eating.*** Rewrite a stronger thesis: _____

✏️ Activity 18: Build It with a Formula

Directions: Use the formulas below to create your own thesis statements. Choose topics you're interested in (school, sports, books, music, current events, etc.). Follow the structure carefully and be sure to make your thesis specific, clear, and debatable when needed.

1. ARGUMENTATIVE THESIS

Formula: Although [opposing view], [your position] because of [reasons 1, 2, and 3].

Example: Although some people think video games are a waste of time, they can actually improve problem-solving skills, encourage teamwork, and boost creativity.

Your turn: Write your Argumentative Thesis

_____

_____

2. ANALYTICAL THESIS

Formula: [Subject] [reveals/demonstrates/symbolizes] [insight] through [aspects 1, 2, and 3].

Example: The song "Fight Song" demonstrates personal empowerment through its lyrics of resilience, its rising melody, and its wide popularity as an anthem of strength.

Your turn: Write your Analytical Thesis

_____

_____

3. EXPOSITORY THESIS

Formula: [Topic] is characterized by [aspects 1, 2, and 3].

Example: Healthy friendships are characterized by trust, loyalty, and consistent communication.

Your turn: Write your Expository Thesis

_____

_____

Developing Body Paragraphs

Body paragraphs are where you develop your ideas and support your thesis with evidence and analysis. Each body paragraph should focus on a single main point that connects directly to your thesis statement. Well-structured body paragraphs give your essay clarity and coherence.

1. Topic Sentence

Begin with a clear statement introducing the main point of the paragraph. This sentence should directly support your thesis and tell readers what the paragraph will be about.

Example: "The COVID-19 pandemic created unprecedented opportunities for quality family time as lockdowns forced households to remain together."

2. Supporting Evidence

Provide specific examples, facts, statistics, quotations, or anecdotes that support your topic sentence. Strong evidence makes your argument more convincing.

Example: "According to a 2021 Pew Research study, 67% of parents reported spending more time with their children during the pandemic, with 52% indicating this increased time strengthened family bonds."

3. Analysis/Explanation

Explain how your evidence supports your point. Don't assume the connection is obvious—tell readers explicitly how to interpret the evidence.

Example: "These statistics reveal that despite the challenges of the pandemic, many families experienced a silver lining in the form of stronger relationships, suggesting that our pre-pandemic lifestyles may have limited meaningful family interactions."

4. Transition to Next Point

End with a sentence that concludes your current point and connects to the next paragraph. This creates flow between your ideas.

Example: "Beyond strengthening family bonds, the pandemic also created space for many people to pursue entrepreneurial ventures they had previously postponed."

Common Body Paragraph Problems

Topic drift: Paragraph discusses multiple unrelated ideas

Insufficient development: Point is stated but not adequately supported

Missing analysis: Evidence is presented without explanation

Poor transitions: Paragraphs feel disconnected from each other

Too short: Lacks the minimum 5 sentences needed for development

Effective Transitions Between Paragraphs

Purpose	Transition Words/Phrases
To add information	Furthermore, Additionally, Moreover, Also
To show contrast	However, Conversely, On the other hand, Nevertheless
To provide example	For instance, For example, Specifically, In particular
To show sequence	First, Second, Next, Finally, Subsequently
To show cause/effect	Therefore, Consequently, As a result, Thus

> Remember that your body paragraphs should work together to support your thesis. Each paragraph should build upon the previous one to create a coherent, persuasive argument. Be sure each paragraph clearly connects to your main thesis and contains sufficient development to support your claims.

✏️ Activity 19: Strengthen the Paragraph

Directions: Read the paragraph below. It contains several *common body paragraph problems* (topic drift, missing analysis, weak transitions, insufficient development).

Paragraph Example (Weak):
Many students like pizza. Pizza is eaten all over the world. Homework is too hard sometimes. Teachers should give less homework because students are tired. For example, I had three assignments last night.

Part 1 – Identify the Problems

1. Where does the paragraph **drift off topic**? _____
2. Which sentence is **insufficiently developed**? _____
3. Where is the **evidence missing analysis**? _____
4. What transition words could improve the flow? _____

Part 2 – Rewrite & Improve

Now, rewrite the paragraph so that:

- It focuses on **one main idea**.
- It has **at least 5 sentences**.
- It uses **at least two transition words/phrases** from the chart.
- It includes **analysis** that explains the evidence.

✏️ **Your Improved Paragraph:**

_____
_____
_____
_____
_____

Writing Effective Introductions and Conclusions

Introductions and conclusions are critical parts of your essay. They frame your argument and leave a lasting impression on the reader. Even though they're often written last, they are the **first and last things your reader will see.**

Introduction Strategies

An effective introduction should:

| Grab attention | Provide context | Clearly state your thesis |

Here are some strategies you can use:

1. Surprising Fact or Statistic

"Over 60% of American adults have experienced a digital privacy breach, yet most continue to share personal information online without hesitation."

2. Relevant Quotation

"As Maya Angelou once said, 'There is no greater agony than bearing an untold story inside you.' This wisdom applies not only to creative writing but also to scientific research that remains unpublished."

3. Provocative Question

"What would happen if every American reduced their meat consumption by just 10%? The environmental impact would be equivalent to taking 10 million cars off the road annually."

4. Brief Anecdote

"When Maria Rodriguez arrived in Boston with just $75 and a suitcase, she couldn't have imagined that twenty years later she would be addressing MIT's graduating class as their commencement speaker."

Conclusion Strategies

An effective conclusion should:

- Synthesize your main points (show how they connect).
- Leave readers with something to think about.
- Here are some approaches you can use:

1
1. Synthesize, Don't Summarize
Rather than simply restating your points, show how they work together to support your thesis.

2
2. Answer "So What?"
Explain the broader significance of your argument. Why should readers care?

3
3. Call to Action
Suggest steps readers can take based on your argument.

4
4. Look to the Future
Discuss implications or predict what might happen next.

5
5. Circle Back to the Introduction
Reference your opening hook to create a sense of closure.

Notes:
_____
_____
_____

> ⊗ **Introduction and Conclusion Pitfalls to Avoid**
>
> - **Vague generalizations:** "Since the beginning of time, people have been interested in education."
> - **Dictionary definitions:** "According to Merriam-Webster, leadership is defined as..."
> - **Announcing your intentions:** "In this essay, I will discuss three points about climate change."
> - **Introducing new evidence:** Don't bring up new supporting points in your conclusion.
> - **Apologizing:** "I'm not an expert, but..." undermines your credibility.

Remember that your introduction and conclusion work together to frame your essay. They should feel connected while avoiding exact repetition. Spend extra time crafting these sections—they have a disproportionate impact on readers' impressions of your writing.

✏️ Activity 20: Introduction Hook Builder

Directions: Read the essay topic below. Then, write two different introductions using two different strategies from the list (Surprising Fact, Quotation, Provocative Question, or Brief Anecdote).

Essay Topic: *The benefits and drawbacks of social media for teenagers.*

Introduction 1 (Strategy): _____

_____

Introduction 2 (Strategy): _____

_____

✏️ Activity 21: Closing with Impact

Directions: Below is the thesis statement for an essay. Write two different conclusions using two different strategies from the list (Synthesize, So What?, Call to Action, Look to the Future, or Circle Back).

Thesis Statement: *While social media helps teens stay connected, it can also lead to anxiety, loss of focus, and unhealthy comparisons.*

Conclusion 1 (Strategy: _____)

Conclusion 2 (Strategy: _____)

✏️ Activity 22: Essay Bookends Challenge

Directions: Think of your essay like a story — the *introduction* is the opening scene, and the *conclusion* is the closing scene. They should connect and feel like "bookends" to your argument.

Below are a few prompts. Choose one and write both an **introduction** and a **conclusion** that feel connected.

Prompt Choice #1	Prompt Choice #2	Prompt Choice #3
Should schools ban homework?	*Is technology helping or hurting friendships?*	*Should students be required to wear uniforms?*

Example (Prompt: Technology & Friendships)

- **Introduction (Provocative Question):** "If you text your best friend every day but rarely see them in person, are you closer — or further apart?"
- **Conclusion (Circle Back):** "Friendship has always been about connection. Whether online or face-to-face, the real test is whether technology brings us closer or keeps us apart."

Write Your Answer:

Introduction (_____):
_____

Conclusion (_____):
_____

Essay Structure: Putting It All Together

Now that we've explored each component of an essay individually, let's see how they fit together to create a cohesive, effective whole. Understanding the relationships between different parts of your essay will help you create a logical flow of ideas.

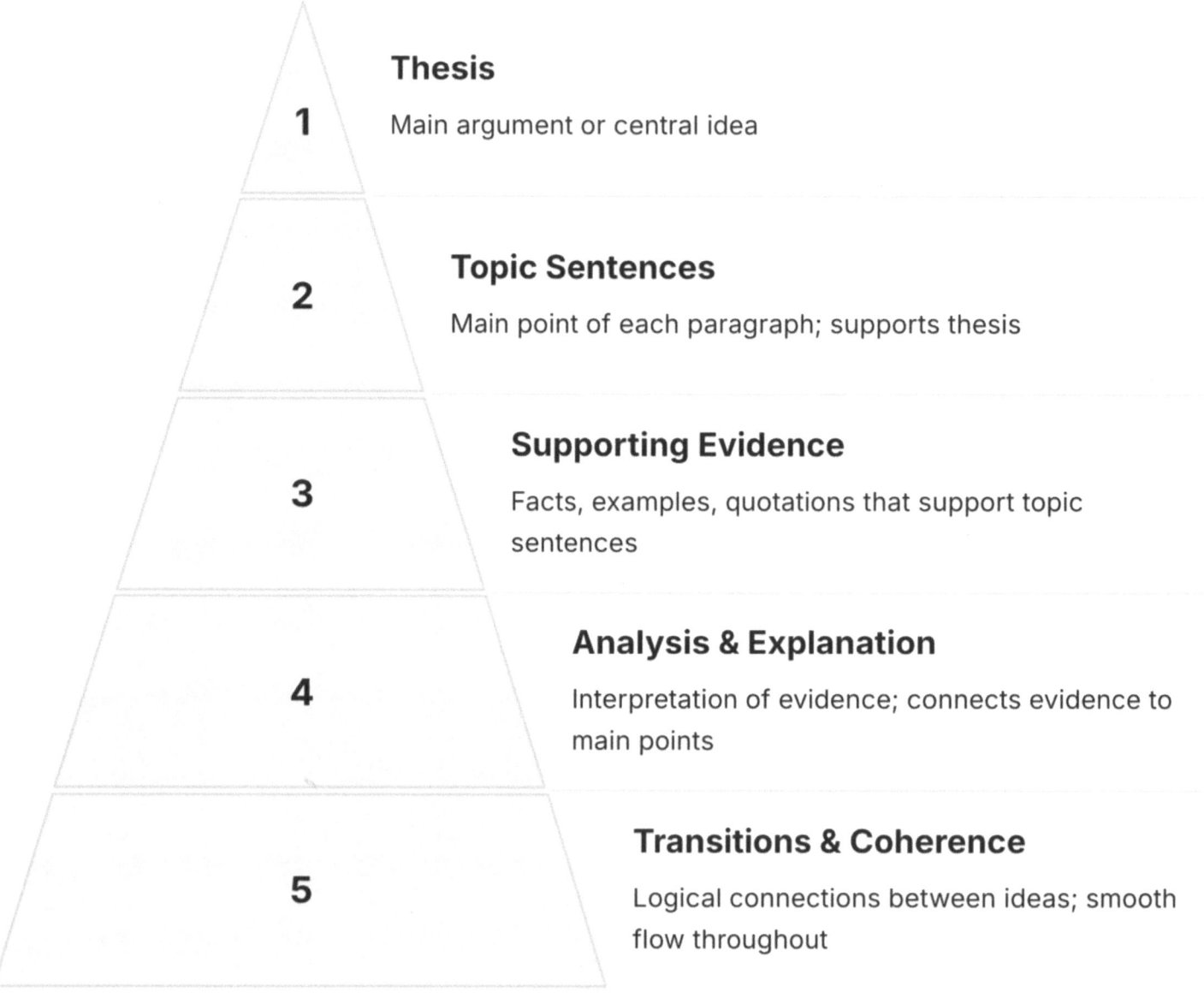

1 Thesis
Main argument or central idea

2 Topic Sentences
Main point of each paragraph; supports thesis

3 Supporting Evidence
Facts, examples, quotations that support topic sentences

4 Analysis & Explanation
Interpretation of evidence; connects evidence to main points

5 Transitions & Coherence
Logical connections between ideas; smooth flow throughout

An essay is more than the sum of its parts. Each element must work in harmony with the others to create a unified, persuasive argument. Your thesis drives the entire essay structure, with each paragraph developing a specific aspect of your main idea.

Sample Essay Outline: 5 paragraphs

> **Thesis Statement:**
> *"The COVID-19 pandemic had positive effects, including more family time, new business ventures, and the growth of remote work."*

I. Introduction Paragraph

- **Hook:** Attention-grabbing fact or idea about unexpected outcomes of the pandemic
- **Context:** Brief background on how the pandemic disrupted daily life
- **Thesis statement:** Main argument or central idea

1 **2** **3**

II. Body Paragraph
1: Family Time

- **Topic sentence:** Increased family togetherness
- **Evidence:** Statistics on family activities
- **Example:** Specific benefits families experienced
- **Analysis:** This shows a positive outcome
- Transition to next paragraph

III. Body Paragraph
2: Business Ventures

- **Topic sentence:** Rise of entrepreneurship
- **Evidence:** Statistics on new business formation
- **Example:** Successful pandemic-inspired businesses
- **Analysis:** Economic and personal benefits of entrepreneurship
- Transition to next paragraph

IV. Body Paragraph
3: Remote Work

- **Topic sentence:** Transformation of the workplace
- **Evidence:** Data on productivity in remote settings
- **Example:** Companies adopting permanent remote options
- **Analysis:** Beneficial for employee and employer
- Transition to conclusion

V. Conclusion Paragraph: Restate the thesis in fresh words

- Synthesize main points (family, business, remote work) as positive adaptations
- Broader significance: How these changes may permanently alter society
- Final thought: A statement about finding opportunity in crisis

Essay Writing Process

Prewriting:
Brainstorm, research, develop thesis

Outlining:
Organize main points and supporting details

Drafting:
Write first version focusing on content

Revising:
Improve organization, clarity, and support

Editing:
Correct grammar, punctuation, and spelling

Proofreading:
Final check for errors and formatting

Remember that strong essays maintain unity (all parts support the thesis), coherence (ideas flow logically), and development (points are thoroughly explained and supported). As you practice essay writing, you'll become more comfortable with this structure and learn how to adapt it to different types of assignments and topics.

✏️ Activity 23: Fill in the Blank – Essay Writing Process

Directions: Fill in the blanks with the correct stage of the essay writing process. Use these words: *Prewriting, Outlining, Drafting, Revising, Editing, Proofreading*

1. _____ is the stage where you brainstorm ideas, research, and develop a thesis statement.

2. _____ helps you organize your main points and supporting details before writing.

3. The first version of your essay, focusing mostly on content rather than grammar, is called _____.

4. When you improve the organization, clarity, and strength of your arguments, you are _____.

1. Correcting grammar, punctuation, and spelling happens in the _____ stage.

2. The final check for errors in formatting, spacing, and small mistakes is called _____.

3. Adding transition words and making sure each paragraph flows logically is part of _____.

4. Coming up with your topic, jotting down ideas, and finding sources all happen during _____.

Sample Essay: Positive Effects of the COVID-19 Pandemic

The COVID-19 pandemic disrupted daily life in countless ways. For many, it felt like the world had turned upside down. Yet, while the pandemic caused great challenges, it also created unexpected opportunities and changes that shaped society in lasting ways. *The COVID-19 pandemic had positive effects, including more family time, new business ventures, and the growth of remote work.*

One positive outcome of the pandemic was the increase in family togetherness. With schools and offices closed, families were suddenly spending much more time at home. A 2021 survey by the American Family Institute reported that 65% of parents felt closer to their children during lockdowns. Families were eating meals together, watching movies, and even trying new hobbies. This increased time strengthened relationships and reminded many people of the importance of family bonds.

The pandemic also sparked a rise in entrepreneurship and new business ventures. According to the U.S. Census Bureau, over 4.4 million new businesses were created in 2020 alone, the highest number ever recorded in a single year. Many individuals used the time to pursue long-held dreams, from opening online shops to launching consulting services. For example, countless home bakers turned their love for baking into small businesses during quarantine. These ventures not only provided financial stability but also brought personal fulfillment to their owners.

Finally, remote work became a major transformation in how society approaches employment. At first, companies were uncertain about whether productivity would remain high outside the office. However, studies quickly showed that employees working from home were often more productive and reported higher job satisfaction. Major corporations like Twitter and Shopify even announced permanent remote options. This shift benefited employees, who gained flexibility and reduced commute times, and employers, who saw lower overhead costs and happier staff.

In conclusion, while the COVID-19 pandemic brought hardship, it also created important opportunities for growth. Families reconnected, entrepreneurs built new businesses, and remote work reshaped the way people think about jobs. These positive changes highlight how society can adapt and even thrive in the face of crisis. The lessons learned during the pandemic may continue to shape our world for years to come, showing us that even in the darkest times, there can be light.

Notes:
_____
_____
_____
_____

✏️ Activity 24: Mastering the 5-Paragraph Essay Outline

Thesis Statement (for reference):
"The COVID-19 pandemic had positive effects, including more family time, new business ventures, and the growth of remote work."

Part 1: Understanding the Outline

1. What three parts should always appear in an introduction paragraph?

1.	2.	3.

2. What is the thesis statement for the sample essay?

_____

3. Which body paragraph focuses on **family time**, and what kind of evidence is suggested to support this point?

- ○ A. Paragraph 1
- ○ B. Paragraph 2
- ○ C. Paragraph 3
- ○ D. A and B

4. In Body Paragraph 2 (Business Ventures), why is an *example* important to include alongside statistics?

_____

5. In Body Paragraph 3 (Remote Work), what is the analysis supposed to show about employees and employers?

- ○ A. Remote work provided greater flexibility for employees (such as saving commute time and balancing family responsibilities) while allowing employers to reduce costs and maintain productivity.
- ○ B. Working from home increased job satisfaction for employees while giving employers happier, more loyal workers, which benefits both sides.
- ○ C. The shift to remote work demonstrated that employees could thrive outside the office and employers could benefit from long-term changes in how the workplace operates.
- ○ D. All of the above

Revising and Editing Your Writing

The difference between average writing and excellent writing often comes down to revision. Few writers produce their best work in a first draft. Effective revision involves looking at your writing with fresh eyes and making deliberate improvements to content, organization, and style.

1

Let It Rest

Set your draft aside for at least a few hours (ideally a day or more) before revising. This helps you approach your writing with greater objectivity.

2

Check Your Thesis

Ensure your thesis is specific, arguable, and actually supported by your body paragraphs. If your essay evolved during writing, you may need to revise your thesis to match.

3

Evaluate Organization

Check that paragraphs follow a logical sequence and that each paragraph focuses on one main idea. Rearrange sections if necessary for better flow.

4

Strengthen Support

Look for claims that need additional evidence or explanation. Add examples, facts, or quotations to bolster weak points.

5

Improve Transitions

Ensure ideas flow smoothly between sentences and paragraphs. Add transition words or sentences where connections aren't clear.

6

Edit for Clarity and Concision

Eliminate wordiness, vague language, and unnecessary repetition. Make every word count.

7

Proofread for Errors

Check for grammar, spelling, punctuation, and formatting errors. Reading aloud can help you catch mistakes your eyes might miss.

✏️ Activity 25: Revise and Edit Like a Pro

Directions: Below are sentences and short paragraphs that need revision or editing. Identify the problem (thesis, organization, support, transitions, clarity, or proofreading) and rewrite the sentence or paragraph to improve it. This exercise will help you apply the revision techniques discussed in the previous section.

Part 1: Identify the Problem

Read each example and write which area it needs improvement in. Choose from: **thesis, organization, support, transitions, clarity, or proofreading.**

Dogs are cool. Also, I like cats. My mom bakes good cakes.
Problem: _____

School uniforms are bad. They should not be allowed. That's what I think.
Problem: _____

I went to the store I bought chips. It was fun
Problem: _____

> 💭 **Writer's Tip:** Fix big issues first (thesis, organization, support), then polish details (transitions, word choice), and end with proofreading.

Part 2: Revise and Improve

Now rewrite the sentences with improvements, focusing on the common issues identified in writing.

Original: *Social media is important.*
Revised: _____

Original: *I love pizza. My favorite color is blue. The beach is fun.*
Revised: _____

Original: *Homework is hard. Teachers should give less homework.*
Revised: _____

Part 3: Apply the Steps

Answer these short questions about your own writing process, reflecting on how you can integrate effective revision strategies.

1. What is one way you can "let your draft rest" before revising?

   _____
   _____
   _____

2. How can you check if your thesis still matches your essay after writing?

   _____
   _____
   _____

3. Write one transition word or phrase you could use to connect?

   _____
   _____
   _____

Extension Challenge – Apply It to Your Draft

Pick a paragraph from something you've written recently (an essay, journal, or assignment).

Revise one sentence to make it more **clear and concise**.

✏️ Rewrite your improved sentence here:

_____
_____
_____

Revision Checklist

Content & Development

- Does my thesis clearly state my main point?
- Do all paragraphs support my thesis?
- Is each claim supported with specific evidence?
- Have I explained how evidence supports my points?
- Are my examples relevant and convincing?
- Have I addressed potential counterarguments?

Organization & Structure

- Is the introduction engaging to the reader?
- Does each paragraph have a clear topic sentence?
- Do ideas progress logically throughout the essay?
- Have I used effective transitions?
- Does my conclusion synthesize main points?
- Does my conclusion avoid simply restating the thesis?

Style & Language

- Have I used precise, specific language?
- Are my sentences varied in structure and length?
- Have I eliminated unnecessary words and phrases?
- Is my tone appropriate for my audience and purpose?
- Have I used active voice appropriately?
- Have I incorporated figurative language effectively?

Grammar & Mechanics

- Are subjects and verbs in agreement?
- Have I used correct punctuation?
- Are all words spelled correctly?
- Have I properly formatted citations and quotes?
- Are paragraphs properly indented or spaced?
- Have I eliminated fragments and run-on sentences?

Conclusion: You've Got This!

Congratulations! You've completed this comprehensive guide to essential writing principles. From mastering grammar basics to crafting cohesive essays, you now have a solid foundation of skills to help you write with confidence and clarity.

Let's recap what we've covered throughout this workbook:

The Building Blocks
We started with the fundamental components of language: parts of speech, spelling, and punctuation. These are the essential tools that allow you to construct clear, grammatically correct sentences.

Common Challenges
We addressed frequently confused word pairs and uncountable nouns—areas that often trip up even experienced writers. By understanding these distinctions, you can avoid common errors that might distract or confuse your readers.

Adding Style and Impact
We explored figurative language techniques that transform ordinary writing into something memorable and engaging. These tools help you express complex ideas and connect with your readers on a deeper level.

Structured Writing
We examined the essay structure, from crafting a strong thesis to developing coherent paragraphs and creating effective introductions and conclusions. These organizational principles apply to nearly all forms of academic and professional writing.

> Remember—writing isn't just for essays and assignments. It's your voice on paper (or screen). It's how you tell your story, share your ideas, and show the world who you are. Every sentence you write is a chance to stand out, inspire, and leave your mark.

Here's the secret: The more you write, the better you get. Don't be afraid to make mistakes—that's where the learning happens. Keep experimenting, keep reading, and keep practicing. Whether you're writing a school essay, starting a blog, creating professional documents, or just journaling your thoughts, every word is building your confidence and skill.

And here's the best part, you now have a toolkit you can carry with you into any writing situation. So go ahead: write boldly, dream big, and never underestimate the power of your words!

Answer Key

Activity 1: Fill-in-the-Blank Story (Answers will vary — check for correct parts of speech.)

Activity 2: Practicing the Remaining Parts of Speech

1. Pronouns: → We

2. Prepositions: → in

3. Conjunctions: → but

4. Interjections: → Wow!

Activity 3: Homophone Match-Ups

break

bear

brake

sell

cell

hear

here

principal

principle

weather

whether

bare

Extension Challenge: (Answers will vary — look for correct homophone pair usage and underlining.)

Activity 4: Build Your Spelling Power

Wednesday mnemonic (sample): → We Eat Donuts Near Exciting Schools Daily And Yearly

Fourth tricky word & mnemonic: (Student-generated – check for creativity and accuracy.)

Answer Key (cont.)

Activity 5: Choose the Right Road Sign

. (period)

? (question mark)

, , (commas)

: (colon)

; (semicolon)

. (period)

: (colon)

. (period)

Activity 6: Fix the Punctuation!

After school we played basketball in the driveway.

✅ Correct: After school, we played basketball in the driveway.

The teacher said "Please put your books away."

✅ Correct: The teacher said, "Please put your books away."

My cousins are here!!!!!

✅ Correct: My cousins are here!

Activity 7: Correcting Uncountable Noun Errors

She baked three loaves of bread for the picnic.

He gave me some very helpful homework.

We heard many beautiful pieces of music at the festival.

The traffic on the road was heavy today.

I need to pack my luggage for the trip.

Answer Key (cont.)

Activity 8: Homophone Challenge

are – We are going to the zoo tomorrow.

its – The cat chased its tail in circles.

affect – The loud noise did not affect me at all.

there – Please put your shoes over there.

They're – They're learning about the Bible at church today.

knew – She knew the song by heart.

write – I want to write a letter to my friend.

pair – We saw a pair of birds on the fence.

waste – Please don't waste your food.

see – The sun will see us through the window.

Activity 9: Figurative Language Match-Up

Onomatopoeia → B. The bacon sizzled in the pan.

Personification → D. The stars winked at me from the sky.

Hyperbole → A. I've told you a million times.

Oxymoron → C. Jumbo Shrimp

Activity 10: Figurative Language Makeover (Answers may vary — check for correct figurative language use.)

Simile: The dog ran as fast as a rocket.

Personification: The storm roared angrily at the town.

Hyperbole: My backpack weighs a ton!

Metaphor: The girl was an angel, spreading kindness everywhere.

Imagery: The candle flickered softly, casting warm golden shadows on the walls.

Answer Key (cont.)

Activity 11: Irony Investigator Worksheet Examples of Irony:

Sentence: The principal proudly announced, "This is the safest school in the district!" Just then, the fire alarm blared—because someone had burned popcorn in the teacher's lounge.

Type of Irony: ✅ Situational Irony

Sentence: Mia spilled juice all over her new white shirt and muttered, "Well, aren't I the picture of grace?"

Type of Irony: ✅ Verbal Irony

Sentence: She told her mom, "I can't possibly miss a single word tomorrow." The very first word on the test was irony—and she spelled it wrong.

Type of Irony: ✅ Situational Irony

Activity 12: Figurative Language Detective Story (Underline and label as follows)

"Break the ice" → Idiom

"She's like a modern-day Cinderella." → Allusion/Simile

"Smell of fresh crayons and the scratch of pencils on paper." → Imagery

"Bright apple, a symbol of learning and knowledge." → Symbolism

"Well, isn't this the perfect day?" → Verbal Irony

Extension Challenge: (Answers will vary — check for correct figurative language type.)

Activity 13: Figurative Language Flip Game (Answers may vary — examples below)

Allusion: The boy was as strong as Hercules.

Idiom: She had butterflies in her stomach before giving the speech.

Imagery: The soup steamed and smelled of garlic and fresh herbs.

Symbolism: The broken clock symbolized how time had stopped for the old house.

Irony: It rained during the picnic on the one day the weather forecast predicted sunshine.

Answer Key (cont.)

Activity 14: Figurative Language Fill-in-the-Blank

(Alliteration) The silly squirrels sang songs on Sunday.

(Pun) I used to be a teacher, but I lost my principals.

(Litotes) That's not the worst cake I've ever tasted.

(Anaphora) I will pray. I will pursue. I will persevere.

(Synecdoche) All hands on deck!

(Alliteration) The bouncing bunnies baked bread by the brook.

(Pun) I used to be a gardener, but my business didn't grow.

Activity 15: The Big Question (Answers will vary — examples of strong, arguable essay topics/titles.)

Phones in Class: A Tool, Not a Distraction

Start School Later: Health, Safety, and Grades Improve

Replace Zero-Tolerance with Restorative Justice

Make Financial Literacy a Graduation Requirement

Ban Single-Use Plastics on Campus

Activity 16: Fix That Thesis!

Weak: Social media has many effects on society. *Strong:* Social media harms teen mental health by fueling comparison, sleep loss, and cyberbullying; schools should adopt phone-free classrooms and digital-literacy instruction.

Weak: Education is important for several reasons. *Strong:* Making financial literacy a required high-school course increases graduation rates and reduces post-graduation debt, and states should mandate it by junior year.

Weak: The Earth orbits around the sun. *Strong:* Because common misconceptions about Earth's orbit cause confusion about seasons and climate, middle schools should add a hands-on astronomy unit to the core science curriculum.

Answer Key (cont.)

Weak: This paper will discuss remote work. *Strong:* Companies should adopt hybrid-by-default policies because remote work raises productivity for knowledge workers, widens talent pools, and cuts commuting emissions.

Weak: How does climate change affect agriculture? *Strong:* Climate change reduces Midwestern corn yields through heat stress and erratic rainfall; federal incentives for drought-tolerant seed and soil-moisture conservation are urgently needed.

Activity 17: Thesis Statement Before & After

Too Broad Before: Sports are fun. Stronger Thesis: Team sports help students build discipline, cooperation skills, and confidence that carry into adulthood.

Too Vague Before: Pollution is a big problem. Stronger Thesis: Air pollution in major cities leads to increased asthma rates, threatens wildlife habitats, and demands stricter environmental regulations.

Just an Announcement Before: This essay will talk about healthy eating. Stronger Thesis: Eating a balanced diet of fruits, vegetables, and whole grains reduces the risk of disease and boosts energy levels for daily activities.

Activity 18: Build It with a Formula (Answers will vary — here are strong examples.)

1. Argumentative Thesis Formula: Although [opposing view], [your position] because of [reasons 1, 2, and 3]. Sample Answer: Although some students believe school uniforms limit self-expression, they actually promote equality, reduce bullying, and save families money.
2. Analytical Thesis Formula: [Subject] [reveals/demonstrates/symbolizes] [insight] through [aspects 1, 2, and 3]. Sample Answer: The novel Charlotte's Web demonstrates the power of friendship through Wilbur and Charlotte's loyalty, Charlotte's self-sacrifice, and the way their bond transforms the farm community.
3. Expository Thesis Formula: [Topic] is characterized by [aspects 1, 2, and 3]. Sample Answer: Successful study habits are characterized by setting clear goals, maintaining a distraction-free environment, and reviewing material regularly.

Activity 19: Strengthen the Paragraph

Part 1– Identify the Problems Topic Drift: Pizza is eaten all over the world. (This sentence drifts away from the main idea of homework.)

Answer Key (cont.)

Part 1 (cont.)

Insufficiently Developed Sentence: For example, I had three assignments last night. (It gives evidence but doesn't explain why that matters.)

Missing Analysis: There is no explanation of why having three assignments is a problem (no impact on sleep, stress, or learning explained).

Helpful Transition Words/Phrases: For instance, as a result, furthermore, because of this, consequently

Part 2 – Improved Paragraph (Sample Answer): Many students feel that teachers give too much homework, which leaves them exhausted and less focused in class. For instance, last night I had three different assignments from three different teachers, which took me over four hours to finish. As a result, I went to bed late and struggled to stay awake during my first class this morning. Too much homework not only limits time for rest and family, but it also increases stress for students. Therefore, teachers should assign a reasonable amount of homework so that students can practice their skills without feeling overwhelmed.

Activity 20: Introduction Hook Builder

Introduction 1 (Surprising Fact): Did you know that the average teenager spends over seven hours a day on screens, much of it on social media? This staggering number shows why we must examine both the benefits and drawbacks of social media in teens' lives.

Introduction 2 (Provocative Question): Is social media a teen's best friend — or their worst enemy? For many teenagers, these apps are a lifeline for connection but also a source of stress and comparison.

Activity 21: Closing with Impact

Conclusion 1 (Synthesize): Social media is a double-edged sword. It allows teens to stay connected with friends and share their lives, but it also opens the door to anxiety, distraction, and unhealthy comparisons. The challenge is not to eliminate social media, but to use it in a way that supports healthy balance and mental well-being.

Conclusion 2 (Call to Action): Parents, educators, and teens must work together to set healthy boundaries around screen time. By using social media with intention, teens can enjoy its benefits without losing focus, confidence, or peace of mind.

Answer Key (cont.)

Activity 22: Essay Bookends Challenge

Sample Response (Prompt Choice #1: Should Schools Ban Homework?)

Introduction (Anecdote): Last night, I stayed up past midnight finishing math problems and reading a science chapter, only to wake up too tired to remember most of what I had learned.

Conclusion (Circle Back): Students should leave school feeling energized to learn — not too tired to think. Limiting homework would give kids time to rest, recharge, and return to class ready to succeed.

Activity 23: Fill in the Blank – Essay Writing Process

Prewriting – is the stage where you brainstorm ideas, research, and develop a thesis statement.

Outlining – helps you organize your main points and supporting details before writing.

Drafting – the first version of your essay, focusing mostly on content rather than grammar, is called drafting.

Revising – when you improve the organization, clarity, and strength of your arguments, you are revising.

Editing – correcting grammar, punctuation, and spelling happens in the editing stage.

Proofreading – the final check for errors in formatting, spacing, and small mistakes is called proofreading.

Revising – adding transition words and making sure each paragraph flows logically is part of revising.

Prewriting – coming up with your topic, jotting down ideas, and finding sources all happen during prewriting.

Activity 24: Mastering the 5-Paragraph Essay Outline

1. Three Parts of an Introduction Paragraph:

    Hook (attention-grabber), Context/Background, Thesis statement

Answer Key (cont.)

2. Thesis Statement for the Sample Essay: "The COVID-19 pandemic had positive effects, including more family time, new business ventures, and the growth of remote work."

3. Which Body Paragraph Focuses on Family Time: A. Paragraph 1 Suggested Evidence: Specific examples such as family meals, game nights, or surveys showing families spent more time together.

4. Why Examples Are Important in Body Paragraph 2: Examples make statistics meaningful by showing how real people experienced new business opportunities during the pandemic.

5. Analysis for Body Paragraph 3: D. All of the above

Activity 25: Revise and Edit Like a Pro

Part 1: Identify the Problem Dogs are cool. Also, I like cats. My mom bakes good cakes. Problem: Organization (ideas are random and not connected)

School uniforms are bad. They should not be allowed. That's what I think. Problem: Thesis (too weak and opinion-only)

I went to the store I bought chips. It was fun Problem: Proofreading (run-on sentence, missing punctuation)

Part 2: Revise and Improve Original: Social media is important. Revised: Social media shapes the way teens communicate, share information, and build friendships in today's world.

Original: I love pizza. My favorite color is blue. The beach is fun. Revised: My favorite things include eating pizza, wearing blue clothes, and spending sunny days at the beach.

Original: Homework is hard. Teachers should give less homework. Revised: Because too much homework causes stress and limits family time, teachers should assign a balanced amount that helps students learn without feeling overwhelmed.

Part 3: Apply the Steps (Sample Answers) Let Your Draft Rest: Step away from your essay for a few hours or overnight before revising.

Check Thesis Alignment: Reread the thesis and each paragraph to confirm that all support the same main idea.

Sample Transition Word: As a result

Extension Challenge – Sample Improved Sentence: Original: My teacher is nice. Revised: My teacher encourages every student to do their best by giving helpful feedback and celebrating progress